THE TWO SYSTEMS OF GOVERNMENT PROPOSED FOR THE REBEL STATES.

SPEECH

OF

EDWARD L. PIERCE,

AT THE

TOWN HOUSE, MILTON,

OCTOBER 31, 1868.

"This is not the liberty which we can hope, that no grievance ever should arise in the commonwealth: that let no man in this world expect; but when complaints are freely heard, deeply considered, and speedily reformed then is the utmost bound of civil liberty obtained that wise men look for."—JOHN MILTON.

BOSTON:
WRIGHT & POTTER, PRINTERS, 79 MILK STREET, (COR. FEDERAL.)
1868.

MILTON, 20th November, 1868.

EDWARD L. PIERCE, Esq., Milton :—

Dear Sir,—The undersigned, citizens of Milton, beg to tender you their sincere thanks for your able and instructive address on the issues of the presidential campaign, recently delivered at the Town House; and in accordance with the general desire, request a copy of the same for publication.

Yours respectfully,

HENRY S. RUSSELL.
J. M. FORBES.
JAMES M. ROBBINS.
JAMES B. THAYER.
JOSEPH M. CHURCHILL.
ROBERT H. BUCK.

MILTON, 21st November, 1868.

GENTLEMEN:—I thank you for the kind terms of your note of the 20th inst., and take pleasure in complying with your request.

Yours truly,

EDWARD L. PIERCE.

To Messrs. HENRY S. RUSSELL, J. M. FORBES, JAMES M. ROBBINS, JAMES B. THAYER, JOSEPH M. CHURCHILL, and ROBERT H. BUCK.

SPEECH.

Fellow citizens, my neighbors and friends.

Had Abraham Lincoln lived to complete his second official term, far different would have been the political condition of the American people from what it is to-day. He commanded the confidence as well of those who had striven to destroy the government as of those who had striven to preserve it. Magnanimous and humane, he would, beyond all other men, have healed the wounds of civil war. But steadfast as the granite of your hills, he would have stood faithfully by the loyal people of the South, of whatever race or past condition. His influence, his great name, his official power, would have been employed to rebuild society in all the rebel territory upon the solid masonry of justice and freedom. The prodigal sons would have returned, sad and repentant, to the old family mansion,—the latch-string still out,—and they and their loyal brethren, forgiving, would have joined in repairing the rents which the war had made. The two races would have come into kindly and co-operative relations. The Southern people, weary with war and politics, would have concentrated their energies on the reparation of their broken fortunes. They would have devoted themselves to industrial pursuits, to the culture of the great staples in larger abundance. Northern capital would have poured into the South, stimulating enterprise and quickening industry. New lines of railroad would have been built, and existing lines pressed on to new districts. As free society tends to a various development, and not like slave society to uniformity, agricultural labor would have thriven as never before, while mechanical, manufacturing and commercial enterprise would have sprung into vigorous life. Manufactories would have risen on streams whose waters had never before ministered to the comfort and progress of man. Ten thousand forges and mills would have been creating untold wealth where now is the silence of the undisturbed forest. The wilderness and solitary place would have been glad and the desert have rejoiced and blossomed as the rose. The wharves of seaboard cities would have been covered with merchandise, departing and arriving. As rights of person and property were respected by public opinion and enforced by law, confidence would have become established; and with this confidence, which is to commercial life what the blood is to the body, would have come ready loans, inflowing capital, and a steady immigration. This new and assured prosperity at the South—this recovery of a disabled member—would have brought health again to the whole country. The honor of the nation and its ability to pay its debts, would have been unquestioned. With a vast production, as yet without a parallel in our history, taxation as well by customs as by internal duties, would have been no longer burdensome. Increased exports would have turned the balance of trade in our favor. The currency would have appreciated to par with gold, putting mercantile life on a surer footing, and reducing the cost of the necessaries of life, to the great relief of laboring and salaried men. With the national credit thus established at home and abroad, the national bonds would have been funded at a lower rate of interest; and thus a controversy would have been impossible which has imperilled our credit, if not our reputation, for national morality.

This industrial regeneration would have modified political antagonisms. There might have been discussion, even earnest discussion, but there would have been none of the heated strife which we now witness. There would have come an era of good feeling, such as was witnessed at the inauguration of the government; such as followed the last war with Great Britain. The good President would have been offered a third term, but, like Washington before him, he would have declined it; and he would have gone back to the home at Springfield that he loved, followed by the benedictions of his countrymen. The people, by a universal instinct, would have turned for his successor to General Grant, who had earned their gratitude and confidence in the field as Lincoln had earned them in the cabinet. He would have been chosen to that high office, not as the candidate of a party, but as the candidate of all the people.

But this fair picture was not to be. The pistol of the assassin changed the course of history. A President succeeded—the creature of an accident—whose wicked and perverse policy fired again the Southern heart, organized afresh the rebel party, and stimulated it with the hope of gaining by craft what it had lost in war. The three years and a half which succeeded the surrender of the rebel armies, have been years of misgovernment, barbarous legislation, disorder, anarchy, persecution of loyal men, murders of good citizens as frequent as once a day in a State, or even in a county; massacres like those of Norfolk, Memphis, Mobile and New Orleans; bands of assassins organized into Ku-Klux clans, and openly recognized as the allies of the unsubdued rebel party. Every morning's newspaper brings a fresh tale of crime and outrage. To-day, instead of being a united people, devoted to the development of our resources, we are meeting such questions as these: Shall there be peace or war in ten States of this Union? Shall protection of person and property, or violence, rapine and anarchy prevail there? Shall the just and liberal governments which have been established there remain or shall they, as demanded by Mr. Blair in his Broadhead letter, and implied in the democratic platform, be overturned by the military and unconstitutional order of the President, and all society be remanded into chaos?

Fellow citizens: The issues of the rebellion are still alive. The forces of the paroled confederates, reinforced by Northern allies, have reorganized as murderous clans and desperate revolutionists. It is another—let us hope, the last—battle of the war. If you have any love for your country, any gratitude to our patriot soldiers, living or dead, any interest in social order, as the father of a family or the owner of property,—whatever may have been your affiliations in the past, and whatever they may be in the future,—your patriotism, your good name, and your safety, all adjure you to give your vote on Tuesday next for the Republican candidates.

Never did soldiers go home from battle-fields with a prouder consciousness of duty done than did ours when, in the summer of 1865, they laid aside their muskets and returned to their kindred and the employments of peace. The military power of the greatest rebellion recorded in history had been smitten to the dust. The nation had been rescued from imminent dismemberment. Its unity, integrity and glory had been maintained. Never before did it rank so high in the family of nations. Despotic dynasties trembled, and oppressed races and classes took heart, as its victory was heralded. Triumphant over domestic foes, over States within itself banded together for its overthrow, it had proved itself the strongest just where friends and enemies alike supposed it to be the weakest. It had won strength and achieved perpetuity in the very struggle in which its doom was anticipated.

But all was not yet accomplished. A work, calling for higher wisdom, and even higher virtue, than the levying of troops, the raising of supplies and the conduct of armies, still remained.

> "Yet much remains
> To conquer still; peace hath her victories
> No less renown'd than war."

The rebellion had, "in its revolutionary progress deprived the people of all civil government." Such were the terms used by President Johnson in his proclamations for the appointment of provisional governors for the rebel States, and for once I can quote him with approval. There were no constitutional officers of any kind,—no governors, no legislatures, no judiciary, no executive officers, no one to receive a vote or administer an oath,—all had been swept into the vortex of rebellion. There had succeeded *de facto* governments, but they were alien and hostile, the creation of public enemies, and they fell with the rebellion itself. It was a *tabula rasa,* just like the slate when a boy has rubbed out the figures of one sum, and before he has begun another. There remained so many square miles of land; so many people upon them; so many State lines, if you please; but no governments. These had been utterly destroyed in fact—not of right, to be sure—by the rebellion, and the fall of the rebellion could not reanimate them. It was necessary upon this vacant, this deserted field, to re-create civil governments,—governments adapted to the changed condition of affairs,—governments which would secure the fruits of the war, and fortify the nation against another rebellion,—governments which would respect and fulfil the pledges made during the war to the national creditors, to the freedmen, and to the loyal white men of the South.

Great as was the work of suppressing the rebellion, the work of restoring civil governments was no less great. Our European friends during the war often expressed misgivings on this point. They said: You may, by your superior numbers and resources, disperse the armed forces of the rebellion, but, after that, whence are to come the loyal hearts which are to uphold civil governments at the South?

"Who overcomes
By force, hath overcome but half his foe."

If you undertake to govern the Southern States permanently as conquered provinces, you will fill your national system with the spirit of absolutism which will destroy your free institutions, as well at the North as at the South.

This was no idle fear. We saw the danger, but we saw also the methods of guarding against it. We proposed the restoration of civil governments based on the loyal people of the South; and these we expected to find in the white men who had been among the faithless faithful found; in repentant rebels who had been swept into the rebellion by a furious current; in the colored population, universally loyal; and in emigrants from the North, and from Europe.

As the result of the war,—of the great upheaval of population, the dissolution of business and local ties, the new spirit of adventure awakened, the extraordinary interest in cotton culture prevailing in all civilized countries, there was anticipated an emigration to the Southern States, no parallel of which has been known since the populous tribes of the North, fifteen centuries ago, poured themselves on the vineyards of Italy and Spain. The war—the accounts of battles, sieges, marches—had instructed our people in the geography of that vast country stretching from the Potomac to the Rio Grande. As our affections and patriotism for four years travelled and lingered over it, places heretofore all unknown became as familiar to us as the hamlets of our birth. Our soldiers, on their marches, their bivouacs, and by their camp fires, had seen the fatness of the land, and had already designated upon it their future homes. Thither thousands of them were likely to go, preferring, after their unsettled life, to set up in business for themselves, rather than to again enter the service of others in the places of their former residence. Becoming thus citizens of the territory which their valor had saved to the Union, they would be like the garrisons which Rome planted in the countries traversed by her eagles. An increased immigration from Europe, attracted by the prospect of profitable industry applied to the great staples of Southern production, was promised. The tide of advancing population had, in its westward course, reached the less available, and as yet less accessible territories beyond the Mississippi, and was likely to turn in a southern direction.

These different sources—the Unionists of the South, white and black; our own soldiers, with emigrants from the North and from Europe—would have furnished ample foundations for a loyal society. Even the great mass of the rebels, under a steady hand, would have proved plastic material. Resignation to the inevitable is a law of human nature; and with that resignation come reflections that, after all, it is a better lot than the one we would have chosen. A strong and just government would have made submission a necessity. A healthy reaction would have succeeded the intense political excitements of preceding years. The pressure of material wants, always controlling in the long run, would have moderated and even extinguished the animosities of section and race. Violent spirits would have disappeared, lost in emigration to Mexico, South America and Cuba, or in retirement from all public activities. The mass of the people would have become disgusted with the agitators who had brought on them poverty, bereavement and dishonor, and would have gathered about new chiefs. Society would have crystallized around the thoughts, the enterprises, and the associations of freedom. The effects of slavery and the rebellion might have been traceable for a generation, but stable and loyal governments, affording reasonable protection to persons and property, would have been possible in one, two or three years. The movement of modern life is so rapid, that what once took a century for its consummation, may now be reached in a decade. What once required a generation, may now be realized in a year. All these reasonable expectations, fondly cherished in patriotic hearts, were defeated by the malignant policy of Andrew Johnson, backed by that portion of the Democratic party which had openly or secretly patronized the rebellion.

But whose constitutional prerogative was it to determine when, how, by whom and upon what conditions these new civil governments should be organized where none existed? Clearly it was that of the loyal people of the country, who had fought the battles, paid the bills and undergone the sufferings of the war. It belonged to them, for they had saved the territory to the nation—not to the rebels who had strained every nerve to wrest it away. It belonged to the whole loyal people of the country as represented in Congress, and through that body expressing their united will and their common wisdom—not to any one man, certainly not to a magistrate, whose business it is to execute and not to make the laws. To frame a government is the highest effort of human wisdom, one that has made the founders of states illustrious in human annals. The American people never intrusted it even to Washington, far less would they intrust it to Johnson. It was the right of the whole people—and as ours is a representative government they could act only through Congress—it was their right to say what was the best time and mode of restoration, and what securities were essential to prevent another rebellion and to fulfil the national promises. It was the duty of the President, hostilities having closed after the adjournment of Congress, to have preserved, by means of the military forces, peace, order and security, through the rebel territory, awaiting the next session when that body in its wisdom might have initiated measures of restoration. If there was any apparent necessity for earlier action, an extra session might have been called. But the President decided upon a far different course. On May 29th, only sixteen days after the last collision between the loyal and the rebel forces—less than seven weeks after his own accession, President Johnson issued a proclamation appointing a provisional governor for North Carolina and providing for a constitutional convention in that State, and shortly after issued others of like tenor for the organization of governments in the other rebel States. He undertook at the outset to say who should be enfranchised as electors—who should be eligible to office—who should form the constitutions and what kind of constitutions they should be. While the conventions were in session he dictated their action by telegraphic despatches. At first, in a telegram of Mr. Seward to Governor Marvin of Florida, of September 12, 1865, he stated that these proceedings were to be subject to the revision of Congress. But subsequently, upon the assembling of that body, he denied its power to alter, revise or supplement his work, and because it would not admit to seats the mere creatures of his usurpation, who styled themselves representatives and senators, stigmatized it as a "rump congress," and "hanging on the verge of the government." As his power to do all this was questioned, he became belligerent, insolent, defiant. This was Cæsarism. This was absolutism of the most dangerous character. No constitutional monarch in our day has asserted such imperial prerogatives. For doing less than this, when you consider the difference of system then and now prevailing, one king of England lost his head and another his crown. The people looked on with amazement at the usurpation. But so apprehensive were they at that critical hour of any conflict between the executive and legislative departments, so reluctant were they to take issue with a magistrate who, a few months before, had received their votes, that they were disposed to submit to the usurpation, provided the governments thus organized proved to be just and liberal, and in that event to overlook their illegitimate, unconstitutional and monarchical origin. The conventions thus called, met during the autumn of 1865 and framed constitutions. Legislatures, in pursuance of their authority, met during that autumn and the following winter, and formed codes of laws. And what was the result?

The first effect of President Johnson's policy, was to reanimate and reorganize the whole rebel element. He had, without interposing any proper period of reflection, without any reasonable pause after the bitterness of civil war, admitted the great mass of the rebels to political power, and had introduced no new force to balance and counteract them. He removed at once all their fears of punishment and stimulated afresh their hopes of domination. Instead of building their fences and working their crops, they flocked to corner groceries and courthouse squares for the discussion of politics. They saw an opportunity to gain by craft what they had lost in war—and they would have lost their nature if they had not seized it. They became self-conscious, aggressive, intolerant. Where there was quiet, submission and acquiescence in May, there was disorder, resistance and defiance in November. Where in May they were resigned to any fate which should be meted out to them as a vanquished party, such as the civil and political equality of the freedmen, and even their own exclusion from political power, esteeming themselves fortunate if permitted to retain their estates and to live in the country, they began in November to threaten another rebellion unless the old masters were allowed unlimited power under apprentice, vagrant and labor laws, to reduce the freedmen to a degraded subordination. Forced to accept the abolition of slavery as a legal statement, they sought to preserve slavery as a social fact. They undertook with systematic violence to drive from the South law-abiding citizens of the North—many of them patriot soldiers, scarred with honorable wounds received in the service of the country, who went there in the exercise of their inalienable right to live where they please. With the ferocity of wild beasts, they hunted down the Union men who had resisted the pressure of treason, and hailed the old flag waving at the head of our advancing armies.

The Johnson governments excluded colored men from suffrage, thus taxing them, but denying them representation. They excluded them from the jury panel, thus denying them a trial by their peers. They admitted the colored witness to testify only in a limited class of cases, a discrimination which had the effect of making him a discredited and impeached witness even when he was admitted. They made no provision for the education of the colored people, save in Florida, thus endeavoring to keep a whole race in ignorance. They undertook upon system by means of apprentice and vagrant laws to revive slavery. Under the apprentice laws, as administered, any planter could obtain the unwilling labor of his former slaves, who were still minors. These laws allowed the judge of probate to bind out children whose parents were unable or refused to support them, giving the preference to the old master; and the courts required no proper proof of such inability and refusal.

The Johnson governments constructed an elaborate system for preventing the colored people from being masters of their time, and for keeping them constantly under the will and jurisdiction of the planters. They made it a criminal offence, an act of vagrancy, punishable with fine and imprisonment for a freedman to leave his employer before the expiration of a term of service prescribed in a written contract. Such was the legislation of Alabama, Florida and Mississippi. It was made a criminal offence in Alabama, Florida, Louisiana, Mississippi and Texas for any person to entice away such laborer, or after he had left his employer to employ, harbor, feed or clothe him. What should we think of a law here, which should send a farm-laborer, failing to carry out his contract, to serve his employer, a year to the house of correction—and which should send there also the farmer who employed him after such breach of contract? Furthermore, under the same Act, every civil officer was required and every person authorized by main force and without legal process to take back such a deserting laborer to his employer, and was to receive for the service five dollars, and ten cents a mile for travel.

In Mississippi, a freedman was declared a vagrant for "exercising the function of a minister of the gospel without a license from some regularly organized church." This was intended to shut the mouths of negro preachers who were disposed to instruct their brethren in the rights and duties of freemen. Another Act of the same State, declared freedmen "found unlawfully assembling themselves together, either in the day or night time," to be vagrants,—thus aiming particularly at Republican meetings and loyal leagues. The same Act declared "white persons usually associating themselves with freedmen, free negroes or mulattoes to be vagrants,"—thus aiming at the teachers of freedmen who taught their children by day and could not obtain board with white families. An Act of Louisiana made it a criminal offence "to enter upon a plantation without the permission of the owner or agent,"—thus aiming at Republican canvassers, teachers of freedmen, and designing to keep plantation negroes in utter ignorance of their rights. In Florida, it was made a criminal offence for a negro to "intrude himself into any religious or other public assembly of white persons, or into any railroad car or other public vehicle set apart for the exclusive accommodation of white people," upon conviction of which he should be "sentenced to stand in the pillory for one hour, or be whipped not exceeding thirty-nine stripes, or both at the discretion of the jury." What think you of that provision, you who for curiosity or information are accustomed to frequent public meetings?

In furtherance of the same purpose to reduce the freedmen to a degraded subordination by attaching them to the soil and keeping them under the constant will of employers, the planters enacted a law in Mississippi, forbidding a negro from doing "irregular and job work" without a license from the municipal authorities; and another in South Carolina, forbidding him from practising "the art, trade or business of an artisan, mechanic or shopkeeper, or any other trade, employment or business, (besides that of husbandry or that of a servant under a contract for service or labor,) on his own account or for his own benefit, or in partnership with a white person," without a license to expire in a year, from the district court. What free society tolerates such functions, in judges, mayors and selectmen? Is a man a freeman, unless he can follow any honest, useful calling that he chooses without let or hindrance?

In Louisiana, the freedman, as a laborer was finable for "disobedience to reasonable orders," "leaving home without permission," "impudence" and the like, as if the employer were still a slaveholder and the laborer still a slave.

In Florida, it was a criminal offence, punishable with pillory and stripes, for a negro to own, use or keep in his possession "any bowie-knife, dirk, sword, fire-arms or ammunition of any kind," without a license from the judge of probate; and a similar Act was passed in Mississippi and South Carolina. The object of these Acts was to make the whole race utterly defenceless, and to put them by day and by night at the mercy of ruffians and assassins acting independently or organized as clans. Does not the Constitution of the United States affirm "the right of the people to keep and bear arms?" And have you not the right to keep a pistol under your pillow for the protection of yourself and family? And has not every other man, white and black, that same right? Does anybody deny that right except Johnson lawgivers and Seymour partisans?

Punishments odious, unusual and excessive, degrading alike to society and to the victims, which have been disowned in civilized States, such as chain-gangs, stocks, whipping-posts, pillories, sale at public outcry to the highest bidder, were prescribed for the freedmen. These you will find in the legislation of Alabama, Florida and Mississippi.

It was reserved for the State of Mississippi to devise the most ingenious methods for outlawing and crushing the colored population. One Act of the legislature allowed the colored man to complain of a white man for an offence committed upon him. Great privilege that! But lest the colored man, destitute, disfranchised, landless, friendless, homeless, should thereby take advantage of white men, who were rich, skilled in organization, and making all the laws, another Act was passed a few days later, that if upon the trial of such complaint sufficient proof were made to the court or jury that it had been made falsely and maliciously, the court should in that very trial impose on such freedman, free negro or mulatto, a fine not exceeding fifty dollars, and imprisonment not exceeding twenty days; and for failure to pay the fine and costs, the sheriff was directed to hire him out at public outcry! Look upon this barbarous provision! I know well enough that just codes provide for the punishment of malicious prosecutions, provisions however rarely invoked in the administration of criminal law. But this is inflicted only in independent proceedings, where the malice is the direct and only issue of the whole case, and where the defendant is shielded by the beneficent presumptions of the criminal law. Never is it and never should it be inflicted on the trial of the prosecution which is claimed to have been malicious. Imagine an instance under this Mississippi Act. A negro enters a county court room to complain of his employer for putting out his eye or maiming him for life. Perhaps he was one of that heroic band who assaulted Port Hudson; perhaps he was by the side of Colonel Shaw as he charged upon Fort Wagner; perhaps he was one of the thirty thousand colored soldiers who made a third or fourth of Grant's army before Richmond in the last winter of the war; or, it may have been he who aided your son to escape from Andersonville, and saved him from starvation and recapture. Whether he be one of these or not, he is at least one whose freedom the proclamation of President Lincoln pledged the government to "recognize and maintain." The injured man looks about him in that court room, but sees no friendly face; no lawyer who cares to breast the wrath of the only class who have money to pay fees. He looks at the judge, and he sees in him a confederate colonel, or worse yet, a confederate editor, too cowardly to fight against his country, and just mean enough to slander her at a safe distance. He looks at the jury, but they are not his peers, all of another race, all leagued to keep him in subjection; the very men who have made the inhuman laws I have referred to. The trial proceeds. The colored man tells his story in broken speech but with truthful lips. The white man denies all, and of course his word is taken. The jury and the judge mean that negroes shall be taught a lesson for complaining of men of their class. They acquit the defendant, and then, as a part of the same verdict and judgment, sentence to fine and imprisonment the negro complainant for a malicious prosecution. My God! The judgment hall of Pilate with a Roman soldiery for executioners, lights up with justice by the side of this Mississippi tribunal!

The ruling classes to whom President Johnson had confided political power, undertook to prevent the colored people from ever becoming proprietors of the soil, in order to make their subjection permanent and complete. Their condition, even if favored by the laws, was hard at the best. They came out of slavery without property, without an inch of real estate, without personal chattels or a dollar in their pockets. They were liable on any day to expulsion from their cabins. They could not draw water from a well or a spring if the planter refused permission. The greatest mistake made by Congress was in not securing to them a fair opportunity to become the owners of small parcels of real estate. This should have been done, not perhaps by confiscation of the planters' estates and the donation thereof to the freedmen, but in the exercise of the right of eminent domain and of the rights of war, enforcing conveyances upon the payment of an assessed valuation. The planters determined that this should always be so; that the colored people should have no chance to become independent of employers; and that they should have no incentive to save their earnings. They therefore everywhere made combinations not to sell them land. Not content with this, they denied them in Mississippi, by express provision of law, "the right to acquire and dispose of real property;" and still further, they provided that no freedman, free negro or mulatto, should ever "*rent* or *lease* any lands or tenements except in incorporated towns or cities, in which places the corporate authorities shall control the same." I challenge you to find a parallel to this legislative enormity in any other country in modern times Let us look at the import of this provision more closely.

The desire for land—to have one spot on earth where a man may stand, and whence no human being may of right drive him —is one of the healthiest and most conservative instincts of our nature. The people who have it are no longer nomadic. They have taken a great step in progressive civilization. Nor can free institutions last in a country unless a large proportion of the population are proprietors of the soil they live upon. If there is any axiom in political philosophy, this is one. I do not affect classical learning when I say—what every student of history will join with me in maintaining—that the fatal hour of Roman Liberty came when the Gracchi, the greatest and best of her reformers, failed to secure for the landless peasantry of Italy some portion of the public domain. "Great plantations destroyed Italy," said the most sententious of historians, Tacitus. Compare, if you will, the agricultural population of Holland, where the farmers own the lands they till, with that of Ireland, where they do not. There is thrift and intelligence in the one. There is waste and degeneracy in the other. So important, so vital to the common weal, has this principle become, that in England, a country where vested interests are accorded a peculiar sacredness, John Stuart Mill proposes an interference with titles for the purpose of obtaining for the Irish tenantry an interest, if only a tenant's interest at a fixed rent, in the soil they cultivate. Fellow-citizens, he is not a statesman, he is hardly a civilized man, who does not recognize this primary, this most beneficent instinct of human nature. How a man loves his home—the hearthstone consecrated by family affection—the tree he has planted, whose fruit he plucks, and under whose shadow he rests—the vines he has trained—the brook whose flowing waters delight his eye and whose music soothes his weariness—howsoever mean and lowly that home may be, he loves it, for it is his own. The noblest burst of British eloquence was that of Lord Chatham, when he said: "The poorest man may in his cottage bid defiance to all the forces of the Crown. It may be frail; its roof may shake; the winds of heaven may blow through every cranny; the storm may enter; the rain may enter; but the king of England cannot enter! All his force dares not cross the threshold of the ruined tenement!" Alas! fellow-citizens, for the country that has not and never hopes to have a population of small landed proprietors clinging to its soil and sharing in its government! Alas for the country that, once having them, has parted with them forever, their farms swallowed up in great plantations and themselves reduced to beggary or driven to better governed and more favored lands! As well attempt to raise the columns of St. Peter's on a pyramid of sand, as to build free institutions on great aristocratic estates. Now these barbarians of the South—they deserve no milder term—conspired by means of laws and combinations to uproot one of the finest instincts of human nature, and to keep a whole race forever landless and homeless. Tell me if these Johnson law-givers have proved themselves fit architects of government.

I have given you fair examples of the legislation of the Johnson governments. The same spirit of injustice—the same determination to degrade and oppress—was everywhere manifest, in combinations against selling land to the freedmen; in combinations to keep their wages down to the lowest standard; in dismissals from employment on frivolous pretexts, just before the harvest, so as to deprive them of all share in the crop; in the unblushing partiality of juries and the lower courts; in the burning of their school-houses and churches; in the mobbing and expulsion of their teachers; in daily assaults and murders which went unpunished and unprosecuted; all culminating in such massacres as those of Norfolk, Memphis, New Orleans and Mobile.

With such barbarous legislation and such prevailing injustice, a neglect of Congress to interpose would have been abdication of a high trust. Nevertheless, it proceeded with great caution; too great, history will probably say. It passed over the President's veto, the Civil Rights Act of April 9, 1866, which affirmed the equal civil rights of the freedmen, and prescribed punishments upon all persons who should undertake under color of law to deprive them of rights or inflict on them different punishments, pains or penalties on account of their color, race or former condition. This Act did something to protect the freedmen in some localities; but as a general remedy it proved ineffective. Two months later, Congress submitted to the States, partly with a view of securing equal rights and partly with a view of testing the loyalty of the Johnson governments, the constitutional amendment, now known as the fourteenth. It was liberal and considerate in terms. It declared the citizenship of all persons born or naturalized in the United States, and forbade any State to abridge the privileges or immunities of the citizens of the United States. Surely none can object to that constitutional truism. It reduced Congressional representation in the same proportion as any State reduced its body of electors by disfranchisement. That applied to all the States, and was certainly fair. It affirmed the validity of the national debt. What honest citizen can object to that? It forbade the payment by the United States or by any State of the rebel debt? Is any one of you specially anxious to pay a share of that debt? If you are, you can buy a rebel bond. It incapacitated for public trust certain officers who, having taken an oath to support the Constitution of the United States, afterwards violated that oath and engaged in rebellion? Is there anything harsh in that? It did not deprive them of life, liberty, property, civil rights, suffrage even, but only of *office*. Was ever treason so kindly treated? It excluded from office a far less number than were excluded by Mr. Johnson's amnesty Proclamation, issued contemporaneously with his appointment of provisional governors. And furthermore, it even empowered Congress to remove this disability by a two-thirds vote, thus making it temporary only, to remain no longer than the exigency. How was this overture of peace and reconciliation met? In the winter of 1866-7, it was rejected contemptuously, rejected unanimously, generally not a single member of either house in the Johnson legislatures voting for it.

Congress at last, pressed by the loyal people, entered on a thorough policy in March, 1867. By one Act it divided the rebel States into military districts and required the President to assign to each an officer of superior rank and clothed him with extraordinary powers for the protection of persons and property. By another Act it prescribed the registration as voters in each State of the people, irrespective of color or race, who were not excluded from office by the fourteenth constitutional amendment. Such electors, if voting for a constitutional convention, were to choose delegates; and the convention was to frame a constitution which upon its ratification was to be submitted to Congress, and if found to be expressive of the popular will in such State and proper in its provisions, the State was to be admitted under it to representation in Congress. Contrast in one item alone the care of Congress with the slip-shod haste of Mr. Johnson. The constitutions framed under the President were not submitted for ratification to a popular vote, but became such upon the adjournment of the conventions which framed them. The governments organized under Congress were all submitted to a popular vote. Under these Acts of Congress, constitutions were formed by the people of the late rebel States. Unlike those of the Johnson governments, they make no discrimination on account of race, color or former condition of servitude, but prohibit such discrimination and secure equal rights for all. They make the most liberal provision for popular education, as broad as any in the statutes of Massachusetts or New York. Never in the history of that section of country have the laws been so expressive of humanity and civilization.

Now, you are called upon, fellow-citizens, to decide between the Johnson governments with their cruel, barbarous and unequal legislation and the governments organized under the auspices of Congress, with their liberal, just and humane provisions. Not only this; you are asked not merely to choose between them, but to say whether you will destroy the good governments and restore the bad governments in their place. More than this even, you are summoned by Mr. Blair, the democratic candidate for the vice-presidency, to allow him and his associates, by military usurpation and violence, to overturn just governments and to set up unjust governments in their place. Was there ever a more one-sided issue? The Republicans are the true conservatives, and they say, Let the just governments now established abide.

But I am told that this whole business of reconstruction, as treated by the Republicans, is made to concern only the negroes, and that they are not our brothers, nor are we their keepers. This is not so. We plead for good government, and that concerns all men for all time. It is not merely a question of sentiment or of abstract justice. It is a question which comes home to the pockets of every one of you. There is not a man here with a shirt on his back, or who expects to sleep between two sheets to-night; there is not a woman here who goes shopping on Saturdays for nine small children; there is not a father of a family who has to fit out his daughter for marriage; there is not one of these who is not pecuniarily interested in its just solution. There is not a bale of cotton, there is hardly a case of tobacco, there is not a barrel of rice or of turpentine, which is not the product of the labor of the freedmen. Go to a plantation in Georgia in early spring, and you will see these freedmen preparing the cotton land for the season; later you will see them—men, women and children—planting it; then hoeing it during the summer; then picking it in autumn; then ginning, baling and carting it to a railroad depot or to a landing place on a river, whence it is to be transported to New York, Boston or Liverpool; all the labor is that of the freedmen. There is the white man's capital invested in the product, and there is sometimes, not always, his superintendence. That cotton, after its manufacture, is to be worn by you and your family; and as good and equal laws prevail at the South, you are to pay more or less for it. What I have said of cotton is true also of rice and turpentine; and it is, though less so, true of tobacco, which is, however, largely planted in the free States. Through, then, these great staples, the freedmen are present in your daily comforts; they supply your manufactures and your commerce; they regulate your balances with foreign nations; they determine the value of your currency; they make and they vary the figures on your ledgers; seen or unseen by you, they are present in your homes, your banks, your warehouses, your workshops, and in all the avenues of your life. Take the single product of cotton. The crop of 1867 was two millions and six hundred thousand bales, worth two hundred and fifty millions of dollars. One-third of it was consumed at home, two-thirds of it exported. Now, if the

Forrests and Wade Hamptons are to have their way with this people; if they are to be the victims of violence, Ku-Klux clans, and massacres, this great production is to be exterminated. These freedmen have once tasted of freedom and suffrage, and before they will go back to slavery in name or in fact, they will resist, as they ought to resist, to the bitter end. It will be San Domingo again, as when Napoleon undertook to reduce the emancipated slaves back to bondage. You will have the horrors and ravages of civil and servile war combined. Where then will be the product to feed your mills, to supply your spindles, to provide work for your factory operatives, men and women, native and foreign-born? Recall the wail of distress which came from Lancashire in 1861, and ask yourselves if you wish to hear it from Lowell, and Lawrence, and Fall River?

But this is not all. You are to have, by this policy of injustice, one-half of all your exports obliterated. The total exports for the year ending June 30, 1867, were $440,838,834. The great item was cotton, which amounted to $202,911,410. Another item was tobacco, amounting to $22,671,126. Another was turpentine, amounting to $1,066,986. Let these branches of industry, conducted mainly by freedmen, be destroyed, and how are you to meet the balance of trade against you? Your currency will depreciate; gold will rise to two hundred; your bonds will fall in the market; your capacity to borrow will be diminished; and your credit everywhere suffer. On the other hand, give peace, security and justice to all races and classes; let your flag be the symbol of protection to all men, the meanest as well as the highest, and your cotton crop will be doubled; your tobacco, turpentine and rice interests will thrive; your mills will be alive with the hum of industry; your currency will appreciate to par; your credit, as well as your honor, will be unquestioned in the markets of the world; and your national debt can be funded at lower rates of interest. Behold the choice! On the one side, just government, with commercial prosperity in its train. On the other, oppression and violence, with commercial disaster and ruin. Which will you have? The Sibyl offers you the precious boon at the mere price of a ballot. Refuse her, and when she comes again, she will demand more than you can pay.

Sometimes, in individual life, seeing the prosperity of the wicked, we almost distrust Providence. But this is never so with nations, whose life is measured by centuries. Spain lived on the plunder of Mexico and the Indies; and where has she been for two hundred years? She now shows the first sign of life in the expulsion of a dissolute and tyrant queen, and in movements for a constitutional government and the abolition of slavery. We lived on the sufferings and unrequited toil of a race for two centuries, and even inventoried their bodies as national wealth. But the furies of Retribution were gathering, and at last they came in civil war, with mourning homes, wasted industry, and a grievous debt.

This injustice and violence at the South, this oppressive legislation and persecution, are to be felt in another serious way at the North as well as at the South. They will force a redistribution of the laboring population of the South, precipitating it upon us. The great mass of the Southern freedmen, driven from homes and accustomed avocations, will come here in hordes, to compete with our laborers in various employments. It will be another hegira. Under the operation of natural laws and the sway of just government, the distribution of a laboring population is accomplished quietly and without any derangement of industrial relations. The law of demand and supply regulates the emigration of human beings, just as it regulates the exportation of products. The surplus flows off from communities and countries where it is too abundant, to communities and countries in which there is a deficiency. In this way, the tide of emigration runs from Europe to America, and from the Eastern States of this Union, to the valley of the Mississippi and the States and Territories upon the Pacific. But there is another kind of emigration forced by persecution and oppression. That strips and impoverishes the country which it leaves, and though it sometimes helps, it often crowds the country whither it goes. How often has religious persecution desolated districts of one country and built up cities in another. Geneva in the time of Calvin doubled her population with Marian and Huguenot exiles. Among the early settlers of South Carolina and New York were large bodies of Protestants who had been driven from France. They were perpetuated in many honored names, and among them those of Laurens and Jay. But take a single period. The revocation of the edict of Nantes, by Louis XIV., which terminated the toleration of the Huguenots, drove from France a quarter of a million of her most industrious, most intelligent and most skilful population. They escaped, spite of edicts and guards, to Switzerland, Holland, England and America. They entered the armies of the continent, and aided in the victory of William of Orange at the battle of the Boyne. Never did a country pay more dearly and more speedily for injustice perpetrated on the weak. Many branches of manufacture were well nigh destroyed in France. They were translated to the countries which offered a refuge to the thrifty and ingenious exiles. Manufactories were closed by the hundred, villages depopulated, large towns half deserted, and the tillage of wide tracts of territory abandoned. The Dutch cloth makers of Abbeville emigrated in a body, leaving none to carry on the manufacture. At Tours, of forty thousand silk artisans, only four thousand remained, and of eight hundred mills only seventy were kept alive. Of four hundred tanneries in Lorraine, only fifty-eight were found in 1698. The population of Nantes was reduced from eighty thousand to one-half that number. Of twelve thousand silk artisans in Lyons, nine thousand fled. The industry of these flourishing centres of craft and trade was so completely prostrated, that they did not recover for a century, if they have completely recovered at this day.

What was done in France under Louis XIV., would be done in the United States under Horatio Seymour. The freedmen would fly to the Northern States for protection, and take their place by the side of our laboring population, native and foreign-born. Remember, too, that they are not merely field hands, producers of cotton, tobacco, turpentine and rice. On every large plantation of the South there is a carpenter, often a blacksmith, and they are colored men. Wherever, too, there is a steam-engine to crush sugar-cane or gin cotton, there you will find a black engineer. And the same is true of other mechanical operations. These people are also pilots and sailors on the sea, as well as skilful workmen on the land. Take a single State for illustration. One-third of the colored men of North Carolina are mechanics. There are in that State five black mechanics to one white mechanic, one hundred thousand black mechanics to twenty thousand white mechanics. They are blacksmiths, gunsmiths, wheelwrights, millwrights, machinists, carpenters, cabinet-makers, plasterers, painters, ship-builders, stone masons, bricklayers, pilots and engineers. You could supply almost any manufactory in Massachusetts from such material.

But you say these freedmen will not dare to come to the North. They had a warning in the riots of July, 1863. Ah! you mistake. The world has moved in five years. Horatio Seymour will not be Governor of New York in July, 1869, as he was in July, 1863. The Governor, whoever he may be, will not go down from Albany to address a mob as "*my friends.*" That has ceased to be respectable. It has cost too many speeches to explain those unfortunate words. The city of New York has paid two or three millions of dollars, quite money enough, by way of damages for such violence. The householders of the city and the insurance capitalists will protest against the relighting of the torches of desperate men. Incendiarism, beginning at the Bowery, might sweep to the Fifth Avenue and to Madison Square. The Anglo-Saxon love of order, the American love of fair play, the human instinct for justice and security will prevent the repetition of these horrors, never to be named without a shudder. No; these freedmen, exiles from oppression, driven from the South by rebel clans and democratic partisans, will be welcomed in the free States with the same sacred hospitality which awaited the Huguenots wherever they fled. Let them come here, if moved by natural laws, but let them not be driven hither by violence to the impoverishment of the South and the disturbance of our industrial system.

Every just sentiment as well as self-interest forbids us to forget the colored population of the South, or to withhold from them protection. There were 178,975 colored soldiers who enlisted for the suppression of the rebellion; of these, 123,156 were in service at one time. The last year of the war they formed about one-ninth of our army. Thirty thousand of them were with Grant before Richmond, holding the nearest point to that city—Fort Harrison. In the presence of yourself, Mr. President, (Colonel Henry S. Russell,) who have commanded colored troops, I need only mention Port Hudson,

Fort Wagner, the advance upon Richmond in 1864, the mine at Petersburg, and the campaign against Mobile. Their services in war are already familiar.

Take their services in another department. One hundred thousand of them at least, were, at one time, connected with our army as laborers. In each of his annual reports, Quartermaster-General Meigs, by no means a sentimentalist, bore testimony to the great value of their services. In his report for 1864 he said, "The negro is not an embarrassment, but a great aid in the conduct of the war." Summing up, in 1865, the work of his department during the war, he paid a tribute to their effective aid, and said: "Colored men continued to the close of the war to be employed and connected with the trains of the quartermaster's department, as laborers at depots, as pioneers with the marching columns. In all these positions they have done good service, and materially contributed to that final victory which confirmed their freedom and saved our place among the nations." Could there be more unimpeachable testimony?

The freedmen were the faithful and intelligent guides of our army during the war. Not to take time in enumerating special instances of this service rendered by them, I give you the testimony of one who has not been a swift witness for the negro in these latter days. Said Mr. Seward, in a despatch to Mr. Adams, of May 28, 1862, "Everywhere the American general receives his most useful and reliable information from the negro, who hails his coming as a harbinger of freedom." Such is the record of our diplomacy.

The negroes were everywhere the friends of our soldiers escaping from Southern prisons. No soldier flying from Andersonville, Salisbury or Libby Prison, ever found his way to our lines, who was not chiefly indebted to them for the means of escape. At much risk, they provided for him food, clothing, boats, hiding-places, and guided him on his way. It was never necessary to approach them with caution, or to inquire in advance who of them might be trusted. The soldier told them his story, and he was safe. Indeed, they seemed to know him and his needs by instinct as he came in sight. The black face was as much the sign and symbol of loyalty as the American flag itself. History records no more touching instances of fidelity than theirs to our escaping soldiers. Mr. Julius Henri Browne, who escaped from Salisbury, has published his account of the obligation of himself and his companions to them. In February, 1864, some thirty or forty officers escaped from Libby Prison and reached our lines in safety. They authorized a published statement of the aid received by them from the negroes, who gave them their only food, guided them on their course, and directed them how to avoid the rebel pickets. Lieutenant Estabrook, of Dorchester, in a most interesting narrative called "Adrift in Dixie," has related his escape from the rebel guard near the southern line of Virginia, his descent of the Dan River, and his safe arrival at our lines before Petersburg. All the way he received constant and cordial aid from the negroes. But why repeat instances? No Union soldier ever escaped from a rebel prison who did not pay a tribute to their fidelity.

There was something sublime in the devotion of the colored population of the South to the Union during the war. Even while the nation protested that it was a war for the Union only, and was not to affect their condition, these lowly people, led by a profound instinct, at dead of night, while the master slept, left their homes of bondage; bearing their children and scanty packs of food and clothing; creeping along the margins of creeks and rivers, beneath the shadow of overhanging branches, in rude dug-outs which their own hands had made; threading forests, pathless except to those for whom the hope of freedom is an unfailing compass; chased by bloodhounds and relentless patrols; approaching rebel pickets at imminent peril of life and capture, till at last, weary, footsore and famished, they cast themselves at the feet of our advanced sentries. They knew, whatever the laws or proclamations or diplomatic assurances might be, God had made them and us allies in the contest. They were wiser in their generation than cabinet or congress. Again, in human history, the truth was hid from the wise and prudent, and revealed unto babes. If we turn our backs upon such a people, we shall receive, as we ought to receive, the execrations of mankind.

It is claimed that this is a *white man's* government, and that therefore the governments established under the auspices of Congress and securing suffrage to all, irrespective of color, ought not stand. Whence came this dogma? In vain will you seek for it in the writings of Jefferson, the great apostle of democracy. He taught the equal rights of all, and man's capacity for self-government. Not one of the fathers asserted it. The Declaration of Independence affirmed that all men, —not all *white* men, but all *men*,—are created equal. The Constitution in its preamble declares, "we the people," not "we the *white* people." It says, we the people, "ordain and establish this Constitution," not this *white man's* Constitution. We do it in order to "provide for the common defence," and "promote the general welfare," not in order to provide for the defence and promote the welfare of any one set or race of men. This doctrine of a white man's government is a modern dispensation. The Dred Scott decision is its creed. Chief Justice Taney is its high priest. You will find its altars in the corner groceries of Kentucky, where the Nasbys, the Bascoms and the Pograms congregate, and where, amid the fumes of Bourbon whiskey, they assume to be the vindicators of the white race. The men that preach it were but too glad a few years ago to find negro substitutes to take their place in a draft.

No, fellow citizens. This is not a white man's government, or a black man's government, or a native born citizen's, or a foreign born citizen's, government. *It is a government of the people, by the people, and for the people.* Our fathers, as they framed it, looking down through future time, saw men of all nationalities, exiles from all quarters of the globe, gathering from age to age under its protecting ægis, and they in their comprehensive humanity ordained that no one of all these, no, not the meanest, the poorest or the blackest, should ever be excluded from the sublime benefaction.

Think not, my friends, that you lower the value of any franchise by admitting others to share it. It is only the lowest order of possessions which must be exclusively appropriated by one. The highest and the best are for all; the air we breathe; the rain that falleth on the just and the unjust; the sunlight which bathes in glory the evening sky; love which setteth the solitary in families; the hope of immortality which shines for all. Do you wish to be alone immortal and live on forever in sublime isolation? Is your wife less precious to you because another has one whom he too loves, honors and cherishes? Is your child less dear to you because some two years since the angel of Life, passing by, dropped a like benediction at my hearthstone? Aye, and when on Tuesday next you cast your freeman's ballot in this hall, are you to prize it the less, and feel your citizenship dishonored because a thousand miles away some Louisiana freedman is to be better protected and have a better chance in life by having a right on that day to cast his first ballot for a President? Shame on you if you do!

The governments organized under the auspices of Congress are stigmatized as "*carpet-bag*" governments. This is a new term, and what does it mean? The facts which gave rise to it are these. Congress authorized the actual *bona fide* citizens of the rebel States, with certain exceptions for disloyalty, to form constitutions, just as the actual *bona fide* citizens of Massachusetts have formed its constitution. Among those actual *bona fide* citizens were a small proportion of persons who after the war emigrated to those States from the North, cast in their fortunes with them, carried capital to them, engaged there in merchandise and the culture of cotton and other products, and thus became as much citizens of those States as if born upon the soil, and just as much citizens thereof as you and I are citizens of Massachusetts. Therefore, they were entitled to the rights of citizenship in those States. The Constitution says, "The citizens of each State shall be entitled to all privileges and immunities of citizens in the several States." These citizens, derisively called "*carpet-baggers*," were in large proportion veteran soldiers of our army; and who had a better right to settle in that territory than they who had saved it to the Union? Now it so happened, and quite naturally too, that the enfranchised colored people had more confidence in these emigrants from the North than in the old planters who had held them and their fathers in bondage, and preferred them in some cases as legislators and magistrates. A number of them were elected in this way to office; by no means a too large proportion. What was there new or strange in all this? Have not qualified electors a right to vote for whom they please, and have not successful candidates for office, duly qualified, a right to accept? But look a little farther. What are we but a nation of emigrants, new settlers, squatters; "carpet-baggers," if you please? What is our government of eighty years' existence by the side of the ancient and august dynasties of Europe? As the tide of population flows westward, the old thirteen are lost in the growing family of commonwealths. In the great city of Chicago, with its two hundred and fifty thousand inhabitants, few of the residents over twenty years of age were born within its limits. People do not ask there "who was your father," but "where were you raised." The citizens of Massachusetts are welcomed wheresoever they go in the new States and territories of the North-West. If any one of you gentlemen shall, a fortnight hence, carpet-bag in hand, arrive in some town of Nevada or Colorado with the intention to make your domicil there, you will be welcomed to the firesides of those who have gone before you; everybody will offer to sell you real estate; and in a week you will be chosen a member of the school committee. Such is the free course of American life.

Now the demand of the Southern rebels is, that the old slave masters should have the exclusive right to occupy and to govern that vast section of country which stretches from the Potomac to the Rio Grande, and from the Atlantic to the Pacific; and that no man from the North, holding other opinions than theirs, shall ever become a citizen thereof, shall ever go there to live, shall ever do business there, or shall ever vote or hold office there. And if they do go there, they are to be stigmatized as "carpet-baggers" and "scallawags," and be driven thence with threats of assassination. What say you to this impudent pretension? We have one country, have we not? divided, indeed, into several States, but still one country, with one constitution, one citizenship, one flag, one destiny. We have a right to go where we please in that country; to carry on any lawful business that suits us; to raise Indian corn and potatoes in Massachusetts or cotton in Carolina; to think as we please; to cast what ballot we choose, and to hold any office to which our fellow citizens may elect us. If we have not these first of all rights, if we have not in four years of blood established them beyond all dispute, if veteran soldiers, scarred and maimed for life in saving that territory to the Union, have not won them for themselves, the sooner we have another war to vindicate them the better.

The Republican party is in favor of paying the national debt according to its spirit as well as its letter. The Seymour party propose to pay it by issuing greenbacks and flooding the country with an irredeemable, inconvertible paper currency which will inflate the price of the necessaries of life; everything which a poor man or one of moderate means, eats, drinks or wears. But who are the national creditors? If they were Shylocks, they should nevertheless be paid what is nominated in the bond. But as a rule they are our friends, not our enemies; those who have confidence in our government and not those who have desired its ruin. The Rothschilds lent the governments of Europe four hundred millions of dollars in ten years, but we asked no loans of them. Our government appealed to the patriotism of the people, who responded with money as they had already responded with men. All classes according to their means subscribed. In time the national bonds passed into the hands of the less wealthy. The rich are more apt to invest in warehouses, merchandise, railroad stocks, factories, ships and real estate. The national bond is an easy investment for a man who has little opportunity or capacity for speculation. Its value can always be definitely determined. It requires no examination of title. It always finds a ready sale. The mechanics of the country have largely invested in the national bonds. So also have the savings banks. Of eighty millions of savings bank capital in this Commonwealth, twenty-five millions are invested in the national bonds. The laboring man and the laboring woman, the journeyman shoemaker and the carpenter, the cook and the seamstress, every depositor in these banks, is interested directly in the preservation of the national faith.

But I fear not the issue of this financial discussion. Every day's debate has driven the repudiators from point to point till now they cry "quarter," explaining that they do not favor the issuing of more greenbacks, though four hundred millions of greenbacks cannot pay off fifteen hundred millions of five-twenties; and they protest that they do not propose the payment of the principal of the bonds till the greenback dollar and the gold dollar are of like value. Why then vex the country with a premature agitation which has brought only discredit? Sorry am I that the Republican party is not quite the unit it should be upon this question. But the masses are right, the organization is right, the declaration of principles is right, the grand current is right. The Chicago Convention denounced all forms of repudiation as a crime and demanded the payment of the public debt in the uttermost good faith, as well according to its spirit as its letter. Vain will be every ingenious or eccentric effort to resist or avoid the force of these plain, honest words. There they stand, and there they will continue to stand as the orthodox Republican faith. Uncle Sam has hitherto been an honest tradesman. He will never consider his creditors paid when he has divided among them fifty cents on a dollar. He ran up heavy store bills in bringing his truant, rebellious sons to terms. He was obliged to take his loyal sons from profitable callings and use them in maintaining family discipline. It was necessary to pay and pension them for their service. Hard pressed on all sides, he was forced to suspend the payment of money for his current liabilities, and to issue promises to pay. He means to meet those promises with money, and not with other promises of no more value than the first. If he is ever in trouble again, he means to carry to the market an unimpeached and unimpeachable credit. God bless the old fellow! Before he would yield to the suggestion of any unworthy child to pay anything else than the real dollar he has promised, the only dollar which the nations recognize as money, before he would have that shameful word *Repudiation* branded on his forehead, he would go to the scaffold as bravely as did John Brown.

It is charged that the Republicans are endeavoring to perpetuate in peace the passions of war. Far from it. Reconciliation, forgiveness, pardon, are the sacred terms of our religion as well as the dictates of a wise public policy. We have not attempted to "draw up an indictment against a whole people," or to "apply the ordinary ideas of criminal justice to this great public contest." We challenge a comparison with the wars against rebellions; and we claim that the suppression of none has cost the vanquished insurgents so little in disabilities, penalties and confiscations. You can almost count on your fingers the estates of which the forfeiture has been claimed. They are less than those which our fathers inflicted on the British loyalists, who, unlike our rebels, remained faithful to the governments under which they were born. There are titles in Milton and Dorchester held under those confiscations. We hold no traitor in prison. We have hung none. Only one man was ever hung for treason in this country; and while John Brown's soul goes marching on, we do not wish to give Jefferson Davis the benefit of a comparison with him which even a common fate might suggest. We have nominated for President the most magnanimous of generals, who has been sometimes censured for his too liberal paroles. We have restored even to political power the great mass of the rebels, only excluding for present security a class of leading men, who had been doubly false, false not merely to the common allegiance due from all citizens, but to the solemn oath they had taken in assuming public trusts. Even these, we are ready to receive back into fellowship as soon as they bring forth fruits meet for repentance, and the public safety admits. We ask nothing for vengeance, punishment, retaliation. But peace, security and protection for the loyal men of the South, white or black, and the fulfilment of our national pledges we will have, cost what it may.

To my foreign born fellow citizens—some of whom I see here this evening—I have a word to say. The mass of you have been heretofore aggregated in the Democratic party. But will you tell me why it is that the great body of you have emigrated to the free States, where Republicans have controlled, and why it is that you have avoided the slave States, where Democrats have controlled? You come to New England and to the Middle States, and you push on to the North-West. But you have shunned the Southern or slave country as a pestilential region. By the census of 1860, there were 4,136,175 persons of foreign birth in the United States. Of these, 3,582,999 were resident in the free States, and the balance in the slave States; eighty-nine per cent. to eleven; eight to one. The State of New York alone had a foreign born population almost twice as large as that of all the slave States together. Of every nine men emigrating from a parish in Ireland to this country, eight went to the free States, and only one to the slave States, and he probably lost his way. Why is this? The answer is easy. Most of you are laboring men, and you want to live in a community where labor is honored and protected. It is honored and protected in Massachusetts, where the Republican policy has prevailed. It has not been honored and protected in Mississippi, where the Democratic policy has prevailed. And again: Republican States like Massachusetts provide free public schools for all, in which knowledge is taught, without money and without price, and in which your children may rise to become Emmetts and Sheridans. The Republicans have signalized the first year of their administration in the South by constitutional and legislative provisions for universal education where none had existed during all the years of Democratic rule. Now will you be false to your true friends, and clasp hands with your real enemies? It is the marvel of our history that you have been heretofore so much consolidated in the Democratic party, whose policy is so adverse to your best interests. But a new spirit is making its way among you. One of the most eloquent voices that ever pleaded for American freedom, for universal freedom, was that of Daniel O'Connell, the great Irish agitator; and young Irishmen now, sharing his tongue of flame, are summoning you to our ranks. Would you secure freedom and justice for Ireland, your first step should be to aid in establishing freedom and justice in America. Remember, too, that when the rights of the meanest and the humblest anywhere are invaded with impunity, the rights of all—yours and mine—are made less secure.

Do we, my friends, appreciate the inestimable value of the votes we give, especially of those votes when they are to establish governments for this generation and for posterity? They are to send influences along the lines of future time, and their end no man can see. Take a single illustration from our history. Upon the admission of Ohio into the Union in 1803, there remained a vast territory now comprising the States of Indiana, Illinois, Michigan and Wisconsin, on whose soil still rested the perpetual prohibition of slavery incorporated in the ordinance of 1787, which Jefferson had drawn. The settlers of this territory, for the purpose of obtaining relief from the scarcity of labor, petitioned Congress for a suspension of this ordinance, and several times renewed their appeal, without remonstrance except once, and they were supported in their petition by Governor Harrison, afterwards president of the United States. Congress, approving a report of John Randolph, as chairman of the committee to whom the subject was referred, refused the prayer of the petition, and again and again refused, although three subsequent committees recommended a compliance. Congress remained firm during the five years that the measure was pressed, and thus saved to liberty that vast territory. Had it weakly yielded, Indiana, Illinois, Michigan and Wisconsin would have become as Mississippi, Arkansas, Alabama and Louisiana; and that great Northern hive, whence issued multitudes of soldiers to defend the government, would have sent forth multitudes to destroy it. To-day we legislate, not for ourselves alone, but for all coming generations. As we sow, they shall reap. As we vote rightly or wrongly, they are to enjoy or suffer. Why, when that child, sleeping in his cradle to-night, tenderly watched by a mother's eyes, shall be absorbed by the activities of middle life, as we now are, he will be the citizen of a country teeming with a hundred millions of people—a country washed by the two oceans and clasped with iron bands, receiving the long-sought wealth of the East, and, if we do our duty, a country dedicated to Liberty, and fulfilling at last the noblest aspirations of the human race. What a responsibility, what a trust, what a duty is ours!

But I must not detain you longer. The Ship of State—pardon the well-worn figure—is now safe. Awhile ago she seemed in some danger from a black craft which, during the war, sailed betimes with French or English colors, and has of late had the names of Seymour and Blair flying at her masthead, and even these she was about to change the other day for others of better repute; but whatever the colors, it is the same old rebel craft still,

"Built in the eclipse, and rigged with curses dark."

As she came up alongside, our Ship, with well-aimed shot from three favorite guns—the Pennsylvania, the Ohio and the Indiana—dismantled and split her in twain, just as the Kearsarge sent the Alabama to the bottom of the sea. Our good Ship is over the bar. She has passed the shoals. The rocks are far behind. She rides in deep waters, bound for the haven of Union and Peace. She is well manned for the voyage. The admiral walks the deck as hopefully and serenely as when he waited for victory before Vicksburg or Richmond. She is freighted with the dearest interests. She bears the hopes of the Human Family. The heavens light up as never before to guide her on her path of glory. Oppressed races and classes take heart and are glad at her coming. Spirits immortal, who ascended from battle-field and prison pen, send down from the skies their benedictions upon her. All is well! All is well!

www.ingramcontent.com/pod-product-compliance
Lightning Source LLC
LaVergne TN
LVHW011128110826
845150LV00008B/2277

* 9 7 8 1 4 1 8 1 9 5 2 6 7 *